50 Best Georgia Cheese Recipes

By: Kelly Johnson

Table of Contents

- Georgia Peach and Brie Crostini
- Pimento Cheese Spread
- Fried Green Tomatoes with Goat Cheese
- Cheese Grits with Shrimp
- Baked Mac and Cheese Southern Style
- Pimento Cheese Deviled Eggs
- Cheddar Biscuits with Sausage Gravy
- Sweet Potato and Cheese Casserole
- Cheddar and Collard Greens Quiche
- Smoked Gouda Grit Cakes
- Pimento Cheese-Stuffed Burgers
- Georgia Peach and Goat Cheese Salad
- Cheese-Stuffed Vidalia Onion Rings
- Southern Cheese Straws
- Jalapeño Pimento Cheese Dip
- Fried Grits Balls with Cheese Centers
- Pimento Cheese-Stuffed Chicken Breast

- Cheese-Stuffed Cornbread Muffins
- Country Ham and Cheese Biscuit Sliders
- Mac and Cheese with Georgia Pecans
- Buttermilk Cheddar Grits Casserole
- Georgia BBQ Pork Nachos with Cheese
- Southern Cheese and Potato Bake
- Cheese and Corn Hushpuppies
- Fried Chicken with Pimento Cheese Sauce
- Cheddar Cheese and Vidalia Onion Pie
- Sweet Corn and Cheese Spoonbread
- Cheese-Stuffed Grit Cakes with Tomato Relish
- Georgia Peach Grilled Cheese Sandwich
- Pimento Cheese and Bacon Dip
- Southern Style Four Cheese Mac
- Cheese-Stuffed Meatloaf with Tomato Glaze
- Southern Baked Cheese Rice
- Cheddar and Peach Chutney Flatbread
- Georgia Boiled Peanut and Cheese Croquettes
- Corn Pudding with Cheese Topping

- Pimento Cheese Pizza
- Smoked Cheese and Grits Breakfast Bowl
- Peach and Ricotta Toast
- Cheese-Stuffed Okra Poppers
- Fried Green Tomato and Cheese Sandwich
- Southern Cheddar Cheese Grits Soufflé
- Grits and Cheese-Stuffed Peppers
- Georgia Peach and Cream Cheese Tart
- Creamy Cheese and Bacon Grits
- Grilled Cheese with Peach Jam
- Southern Style Cheese-Stuffed Waffles
- Buttermilk and Cheese Drop Biscuits
- Pimento Cheese-Stuffed Mushrooms
- Cheese and Sausage Breakfast Grits Bake

Georgia Peach and Brie Crostini

Ingredients:

- 1 baguette, sliced
- 1–2 ripe peaches, thinly sliced
- 6 oz brie, sliced
- Honey, for drizzling
- Fresh thyme or basil (optional)

Instructions:

1. Toast baguette slices under the broiler or in a toaster oven.
2. Top each with a slice of brie and a peach slice.
3. Return to broiler just until brie melts (1–2 minutes).
4. Drizzle with honey and garnish with herbs.

Pimento Cheese Spread

Ingredients:

- 2 cups shredded sharp cheddar
- ½ cup mayonnaise
- 1 (4 oz) jar diced pimentos, drained
- ½ tsp garlic powder
- ½ tsp onion powder
- Salt and pepper to taste

Instructions:

1. Combine all ingredients in a bowl.
2. Mix well until creamy and smooth.
3. Chill before serving with crackers or veggies.

Fried Green Tomatoes with Goat Cheese

Ingredients:

- 2 green tomatoes, sliced
- ½ cup cornmeal
- ½ cup flour
- 1 egg + 2 tbsp milk
- Oil for frying
- 4 oz goat cheese, softened

Instructions:

1. Heat oil in a skillet.
2. Dip tomato slices in egg mixture, then dredge in combined flour and cornmeal.
3. Fry until golden brown on both sides.
4. Top with dollops of goat cheese before serving.

Cheese Grits with Shrimp

Ingredients:

- 1 cup stone-ground grits
- 4 cups water or stock
- 1 cup shredded cheddar
- ½ cup cream
- 1 lb shrimp, peeled and deveined
- 2 cloves garlic, minced
- 2 tbsp butter
- Cajun seasoning

Instructions:

1. Cook grits in water until tender, then stir in cheese and cream.
2. Sauté shrimp with butter, garlic, and seasoning.
3. Serve shrimp over cheese grits.

Baked Mac and Cheese Southern Style

Ingredients:

- 1 lb elbow macaroni
- 3 cups shredded cheddar (plus extra for topping)
- 2 cups milk
- 2 eggs
- ½ stick butter
- Salt and pepper

Instructions:

1. Cook macaroni, drain. Preheat oven to 350°F (175°C).
2. Mix macaroni with butter, cheese, milk, eggs, salt and pepper.
3. Pour into a greased baking dish, top with extra cheese.
4. Bake 30–35 minutes until bubbly and golden.

Pimento Cheese Deviled Eggs

Ingredients:

- 6 hard-boiled eggs, halved
- ¼ cup pimento cheese
- 1 tbsp mayonnaise
- Paprika for garnish

Instructions:

1. Remove yolks and mash with pimento cheese and mayo.
2. Pipe or spoon filling into egg whites.
3. Sprinkle with paprika.

Cheddar Biscuits with Sausage Gravy

Ingredients:

Biscuits:

- 2 cups flour
- 1 tbsp baking powder
- ½ tsp salt
- ½ cup butter, cold
- 1 cup shredded cheddar
- ¾ cup milk

Gravy:

- ½ lb breakfast sausage
- 3 tbsp flour
- 2 cups milk
- Salt and pepper

Instructions:

1. For biscuits: Mix dry ingredients, cut in butter, add cheese and milk, form dough. Cut and bake at 425°F (220°C) for 12–15 mins.
2. For gravy: Cook sausage, sprinkle flour over it, stir, and add milk. Cook until thick.
3. Serve gravy over warm biscuits.

Sweet Potato and Cheese Casserole

Ingredients:

- 3 cups mashed sweet potatoes
- 1 cup shredded sharp cheddar
- 2 eggs
- ½ cup milk
- Salt, pepper, nutmeg to taste

Instructions:

1. Preheat oven to 350°F (175°C).
2. Mix all ingredients until smooth.
3. Pour into greased dish, top with extra cheese if desired.
4. Bake 30 minutes until set and lightly golden.

Cheddar and Collard Greens Quiche

Ingredients:

- 1 pie crust (store-bought or homemade)
- 1 cup cooked collard greens, chopped
- 1 ½ cups shredded sharp cheddar
- 4 eggs
- 1 cup milk or half-and-half
- Salt, pepper, and a pinch of nutmeg

Instructions:

1. Preheat oven to 375°F (190°C).
2. Press crust into a pie dish and pre-bake for 10 minutes.
3. Whisk eggs, milk, seasoning. Add greens and cheddar.
4. Pour into crust and bake 35–40 minutes until set and golden.

Smoked Gouda Grit Cakes

Ingredients:

- 1 cup grits
- 3 cups water or broth
- 1 ½ cups shredded smoked gouda
- 2 tbsp butter
- Salt and pepper
- Oil for frying

Instructions:

1. Cook grits until thick. Stir in cheese, butter, and seasonings.
2. Pour into a greased dish and chill until firm.
3. Cut into cakes and pan-fry until golden on both sides.

Pimento Cheese-Stuffed Burgers

Ingredients:

- 1 ½ lbs ground beef
- 1 cup pimento cheese
- Salt and pepper
- Buns and toppings of choice

Instructions:

1. Form 8 thin burger patties. Place pimento cheese on 4, then top with other 4 and seal edges.
2. Grill or pan-cook until desired doneness.
3. Serve on buns with your favorite toppings.

Georgia Peach and Goat Cheese Salad

Ingredients:

- Mixed greens
- 1–2 ripe peaches, sliced
- 4 oz goat cheese, crumbled
- ¼ cup pecans, toasted
- Balsamic vinaigrette

Instructions:

1. Assemble greens, peach slices, goat cheese, and pecans.
2. Drizzle with vinaigrette just before serving.

Cheese-Stuffed Vidalia Onion Rings

Ingredients:

- 2 large Vidalia onions
- Mozzarella sticks or shredded cheese
- 1 cup flour
- 2 eggs
- 1 cup breadcrumbs
- Oil for frying

Instructions:

1. Slice onions into rings and pair rings to make space for cheese.
2. Stuff cheese between paired rings, freeze 30 minutes.
3. Dredge in flour, dip in eggs, coat in breadcrumbs.
4. Fry until golden and cheese is melted.

Southern Cheese Straws

Ingredients:

- 2 cups shredded sharp cheddar
- 1 ½ cups all-purpose flour
- ½ cup butter, softened
- ½ tsp cayenne (optional)
- Salt to taste

Instructions:

1. Mix all ingredients into a dough.
2. Roll into logs or pipe through a star tip.
3. Bake at 350°F (175°C) for 12–15 minutes until golden.

Jalapeño Pimento Cheese Dip

Ingredients:

- 2 cups shredded cheddar
- ½ cup mayonnaise
- ½ cup diced pimentos
- 1–2 jalapeños, minced
- ¼ tsp garlic powder
- Salt to taste

Instructions:

1. Mix all ingredients until creamy.
2. Chill before serving with crackers, chips, or veggies.

Fried Grits Balls with Cheese Centers

Ingredients:

- 1 cup cooked grits (chilled)
- ½ cup shredded cheese (cheddar or gouda)
- 1 egg
- 1 cup breadcrumbs
- Oil for frying

Instructions:

1. Scoop grits, flatten slightly, place cheese in center, and form into balls.
2. Roll in beaten egg, then breadcrumbs.
3. Fry until golden brown and crisp.

Pimento Cheese-Stuffed Chicken Breast

Ingredients:

- 4 boneless, skinless chicken breasts
- 1 cup pimento cheese
- Salt and pepper
- 1 tbsp olive oil

Instructions:

1. Preheat oven to 375°F (190°C).
2. Slice a pocket into each chicken breast.
3. Stuff each pocket with pimento cheese and secure with toothpicks.
4. Season with salt and pepper.
5. Heat oil in skillet over medium heat; brown chicken 3-4 minutes per side.
6. Transfer to oven and bake 20-25 minutes until cooked through.

Cheese-Stuffed Cornbread Muffins

Ingredients:

- 1 cup cornmeal
- 1 cup flour
- 1 tbsp baking powder
- 1 tsp salt
- 1 cup milk
- 1 egg
- ½ cup melted butter
- 1 cup shredded cheddar
- ½ cup cream cheese, cubed

Instructions:

1. Preheat oven to 400°F (200°C).
2. Mix dry ingredients; stir in milk, egg, butter, and cheddar.
3. Spoon batter into greased muffin tin halfway, add cream cheese cubes, cover with more batter.
4. Bake 15-20 minutes until golden.

Country Ham and Cheese Biscuit Sliders

Ingredients:

- 12 small biscuits (homemade or store-bought)
- 8 oz sliced country ham
- 1 cup sharp cheddar slices
- 2 tbsp butter, melted
- 1 tbsp Dijon mustard (optional)

Instructions:

1. Preheat oven to 350°F (175°C).
2. Split biscuits and spread mustard if using.
3. Layer ham and cheddar, then top with biscuit tops.
4. Brush with melted butter and bake 10-15 minutes until cheese melts.

Mac and Cheese with Georgia Pecans

Ingredients:

- 1 lb elbow macaroni
- 3 cups shredded sharp cheddar
- 2 cups milk
- 3 tbsp butter
- 3 tbsp flour
- 1 cup chopped toasted Georgia pecans
- Salt and pepper

Instructions:

1. Cook macaroni and drain.
2. Make a roux: melt butter, whisk in flour, cook 2 minutes.
3. Gradually whisk in milk; cook until thickened.
4. Stir in cheese until melted.
5. Mix cheese sauce with pasta and pecans.
6. Transfer to baking dish and bake at 350°F for 20 minutes.

Buttermilk Cheddar Grits Casserole

Ingredients:

- 1 cup grits
- 4 cups buttermilk
- 1 ½ cups shredded cheddar
- 2 eggs
- Salt and pepper

Instructions:

1. Preheat oven to 350°F (175°C).
2. Cook grits in buttermilk until thick.
3. Stir in cheese, eggs, salt, and pepper.
4. Pour into greased casserole dish and bake 25-30 minutes until set.

Georgia BBQ Pork Nachos with Cheese

Ingredients:

- Tortilla chips
- 2 cups shredded BBQ pulled pork
- 2 cups shredded cheddar
- ½ cup jalapeños, sliced
- Sour cream and chopped green onions for topping

Instructions:

1. Preheat oven to 375°F (190°C).
2. Layer chips on a baking sheet, top with pork, cheese, and jalapeños.
3. Bake 10 minutes until cheese melts.
4. Serve topped with sour cream and green onions.

Southern Cheese and Potato Bake

Ingredients:

- 4 cups thinly sliced potatoes
- 2 cups shredded cheddar
- 1 cup heavy cream
- 1 onion, thinly sliced
- Salt, pepper, and paprika

Instructions:

1. Preheat oven to 375°F (190°C).
2. Layer potatoes, onions, and cheese in a greased dish, seasoning each layer.
3. Pour cream over top.
4. Cover with foil and bake 45 minutes; uncover and bake 15 more until golden.

Cheese and Corn Hushpuppies

Ingredients:

- 1 cup cornmeal
- ½ cup flour
- 1 tsp baking powder
- 1 tsp sugar
- 1 cup corn kernels (fresh or frozen)
- 1 cup shredded cheddar
- 1 egg
- ½ cup milk
- Oil for frying

Instructions:

1. Mix dry ingredients, add corn, cheese, egg, and milk to form batter.
2. Heat oil to 350°F (175°C).
3. Drop spoonfuls of batter into hot oil and fry until golden (3-4 minutes).
4. Drain on paper towels.

Fried Chicken with Pimento Cheese Sauce

Ingredients:

- Fried chicken pieces (homemade or store-bought)
- 1 cup pimento cheese
- ½ cup mayonnaise
- 1 tbsp hot sauce (optional)

Instructions:

1. Mix pimento cheese, mayo, and hot sauce for a creamy sauce.
2. Serve fried chicken topped or dipped in pimento cheese sauce.

Cheddar Cheese and Vidalia Onion Pie

Ingredients:

- 1 pie crust
- 2 large Vidalia onions, thinly sliced
- 1 ½ cups shredded sharp cheddar
- 3 eggs
- 1 cup heavy cream
- Salt and pepper
- 1 tbsp butter

Instructions:

1. Preheat oven to 375°F (190°C).
2. Sauté onions in butter until soft and translucent.
3. In a bowl, whisk eggs and cream, season with salt and pepper.
4. Place pie crust in a pie dish, layer onions and cheddar inside.
5. Pour egg mixture over the filling.
6. Bake 35-40 minutes until set and golden on top.

Sweet Corn and Cheese Spoonbread

Ingredients:

- 1 cup cornmeal
- 1 cup corn kernels (fresh or frozen)
- 2 cups milk
- 1 cup shredded cheddar cheese
- 3 eggs
- 2 tbsp butter, melted
- 1 tbsp sugar
- 1 tsp baking powder
- Salt to taste

Instructions:

1. Preheat oven to 375°F (190°C).
2. Heat milk and add cornmeal, stir until thickened.
3. In a bowl, beat eggs, sugar, baking powder, and melted butter.
4. Mix in cornmeal mixture, corn kernels, and cheese.
5. Pour into a greased baking dish and bake for 40-45 minutes.

Cheese-Stuffed Grit Cakes with Tomato Relish

Ingredients for Grit Cakes:

- 1 cup grits
- 4 cups water
- 1 cup shredded cheddar
- Salt and pepper
- Oil for frying

For Tomato Relish:

- 2 cups chopped tomatoes
- 1 small onion, finely chopped
- 1 tbsp vinegar
- 1 tsp sugar
- Salt and pepper

Instructions:

1. Cook grits in water with salt until thick.
2. Stir in cheddar and season.
3. Pour into a pan to cool and firm up.
4. Cut into squares, then fry in hot oil until golden.

5. For relish, mix all ingredients and let sit. Serve grit cakes topped with tomato relish.

Georgia Peach Grilled Cheese Sandwich

Ingredients:

- 2 slices of bread
- 2 tbsp butter
- 2 slices cheddar cheese
- 4-5 thin slices fresh Georgia peach
- Honey (optional)

Instructions:

1. Butter one side of each bread slice.
2. Place one slice, butter side down, on skillet over medium heat.
3. Layer cheese and peaches, drizzle with honey if desired.
4. Top with other bread slice, butter side up.
5. Grill until golden and cheese melts, flipping once.

Pimento Cheese and Bacon Dip

Ingredients:

- 1 cup pimento cheese
- 4 slices cooked bacon, crumbled
- ½ cup cream cheese, softened
- ¼ cup mayonnaise
- 1 tsp hot sauce (optional)

Instructions:

1. Mix all ingredients until smooth and well combined.
2. Serve chilled or warmed with crackers or veggies.

Southern Style Four Cheese Mac

Ingredients:

- 1 lb elbow macaroni
- 1 cup sharp cheddar
- 1 cup mozzarella
- ½ cup gouda
- ½ cup parmesan
- 3 cups milk
- 3 tbsp butter
- 3 tbsp flour
- Salt and pepper

Instructions:

1. Cook macaroni and drain.
2. Make cheese sauce: melt butter, whisk in flour, cook 2 minutes.
3. Gradually add milk, stirring until thickened.
4. Add all cheeses and stir until melted.
5. Mix cheese sauce with macaroni, season, and bake at 350°F (175°C) for 20 minutes.

Cheese-Stuffed Meatloaf with Tomato Glaze

Ingredients:

- 1 lb ground beef
- 1 lb ground pork
- 1 cup breadcrumbs
- 2 eggs
- 1 small onion, finely chopped
- 1 cup shredded cheddar or mozzarella
- Salt and pepper
- ½ cup ketchup
- 2 tbsp brown sugar
- 1 tbsp vinegar

Instructions:

1. Preheat oven to 350°F (175°C).
2. Mix meats, breadcrumbs, eggs, onion, salt, and pepper.
3. Form half the mixture into a loaf on a baking sheet.
4. Add cheese in the center, then cover with remaining meat mixture.
5. Mix ketchup, sugar, and vinegar; brush on top.
6. Bake 1 hour or until cooked through.

Southern Baked Cheese Rice

Ingredients:

- 2 cups cooked white rice
- 1 ½ cups shredded sharp cheddar
- 1 cup milk
- 1 egg
- ½ cup sour cream
- Salt and pepper
- 1 tbsp butter

Instructions:

1. Preheat oven to 350°F (175°C).
2. Mix rice, half the cheese, milk, egg, sour cream, salt, and pepper.
3. Pour into a buttered baking dish.
4. Sprinkle remaining cheese on top.
5. Bake 25-30 minutes until golden and bubbly.

Cheddar and Peach Chutney Flatbread

Ingredients:

- 1 flatbread or naan
- 1 cup shredded sharp cheddar
- ½ cup peach chutney
- Fresh thyme or rosemary (optional)

Instructions:

1. Preheat oven to 400°F (200°C).
2. Spread peach chutney evenly over flatbread.
3. Sprinkle cheddar cheese on top.
4. Add fresh thyme if desired.
5. Bake 8-10 minutes until cheese melts and crust is crisp.

Georgia Boiled Peanut and Cheese Croquettes

Ingredients:

- 1 cup boiled peanuts, chopped
- 1 cup shredded cheddar cheese
- 1 cup mashed potatoes
- 1 egg
- ½ cup breadcrumbs
- Oil for frying

Instructions:

1. Mix boiled peanuts, cheese, mashed potatoes, and egg.
2. Form into small croquettes and coat with breadcrumbs.
3. Heat oil and fry until golden brown.
4. Drain on paper towels and serve warm.

Corn Pudding with Cheese Topping

Ingredients:

- 3 cups fresh or frozen corn kernels
- 1 cup milk
- 2 eggs
- ¼ cup sugar
- 2 tbsp flour
- 1 tsp baking powder
- 1 cup shredded cheddar cheese
- Salt and pepper

Instructions:

1. Preheat oven to 350°F (175°C).
2. Blend corn, milk, eggs, sugar, flour, baking powder, salt, and pepper until smooth.
3. Pour into a greased baking dish.
4. Sprinkle cheddar cheese on top.
5. Bake 40-45 minutes until set and golden.

Pimento Cheese Pizza

Ingredients:

- Pizza dough
- 1 cup pimento cheese spread
- 1 cup shredded mozzarella
- Sliced green onions
- Optional: cooked bacon bits

Instructions:

1. Preheat oven to 450°F (230°C).
2. Roll out dough and spread pimento cheese evenly.
3. Sprinkle mozzarella and green onions on top.
4. Add bacon bits if desired.
5. Bake 12-15 minutes until crust is golden and cheese bubbly.

Smoked Cheese and Grits Breakfast Bowl

Ingredients:

- 1 cup cooked grits
- ½ cup smoked cheese, shredded
- 2 eggs, cooked to preference
- 2 slices bacon, cooked and crumbled
- Salt and pepper

Instructions:

1. Stir smoked cheese into hot cooked grits.
2. Season with salt and pepper.
3. Top with eggs and bacon.
4. Serve warm.

Peach and Ricotta Toast

Ingredients:

- 2 slices of bread, toasted
- ½ cup ricotta cheese
- 1 fresh Georgia peach, thinly sliced
- Honey for drizzling
- Fresh basil leaves (optional)

Instructions:

1. Spread ricotta on toasted bread.
2. Layer peach slices on top.
3. Drizzle with honey.
4. Garnish with basil if desired.

Cheese-Stuffed Okra Poppers

Ingredients:

- 12 large okra pods
- ½ cup cream cheese
- ½ cup shredded cheddar
- 1 tsp Cajun seasoning
- 1 cup breadcrumbs
- Oil for frying

Instructions:

1. Cut okra lengthwise, scoop out seeds gently to create a cavity.
2. Mix cream cheese, cheddar, and Cajun seasoning.
3. Stuff mixture into okra pods.
4. Coat with breadcrumbs.
5. Fry until golden and crispy. Drain and serve.

Fried Green Tomato and Cheese Sandwich

Ingredients:

- 4 slices green tomatoes
- 4 slices bread
- 4 slices cheddar or pepper jack cheese
- 1 cup cornmeal
- 1 cup buttermilk
- Oil for frying
- Lettuce and mayo (optional)

Instructions:

1. Dip tomato slices in buttermilk, then coat with cornmeal.
2. Fry in hot oil until crispy and golden.
3. Assemble sandwich: bread, fried tomatoes, cheese, lettuce, and mayo.
4. Grill sandwich until cheese melts and bread is toasted.

Southern Cheddar Cheese Grits Soufflé

Ingredients:

- 1 cup cooked grits
- 1 cup shredded sharp cheddar cheese
- 3 eggs, separated
- ¼ cup milk
- 2 tbsp butter
- Salt and pepper

Instructions:

1. Preheat oven to 375°F (190°C).
2. In a bowl, mix warm grits, cheddar, egg yolks, milk, butter, salt, and pepper.
3. Beat egg whites until stiff peaks form.
4. Gently fold egg whites into grits mixture.
5. Pour into greased soufflé dish and bake for 25-30 minutes until puffed and golden.

Grits and Cheese-Stuffed Peppers

Ingredients:

- 4 large bell peppers, tops cut off and seeded
- 1 cup cooked grits
- 1 cup shredded cheddar cheese
- ½ cup cooked bacon bits
- 2 green onions, chopped
- Salt and pepper

Instructions:

1. Preheat oven to 375°F (190°C).
2. Mix grits, cheese, bacon, green onions, salt, and pepper.
3. Stuff mixture into peppers.
4. Place peppers in baking dish, cover with foil, and bake for 30-35 minutes until peppers are tender.

Georgia Peach and Cream Cheese Tart

Ingredients:

- 1 pie crust (store-bought or homemade)
- 8 oz cream cheese, softened
- ¼ cup sugar
- 1 tsp vanilla extract
- 2-3 fresh Georgia peaches, thinly sliced
- 1 tbsp honey

Instructions:

1. Preheat oven to 350°F (175°C).
2. Beat cream cheese, sugar, and vanilla until smooth.
3. Spread mixture evenly on pie crust.
4. Arrange peach slices on top.
5. Bake 30-35 minutes until crust is golden.
6. Drizzle honey over tart before serving.

Creamy Cheese and Bacon Grits

Ingredients:

- 1 cup grits
- 4 cups water or broth
- 1 cup shredded cheddar cheese
- 4 slices cooked bacon, crumbled
- 2 tbsp butter
- Salt and pepper

Instructions:

1. Cook grits according to package instructions.
2. Stir in butter, cheese, and bacon.
3. Season with salt and pepper.
4. Serve hot.

Grilled Cheese with Peach Jam

Ingredients:

- 2 slices bread
- 2 tbsp peach jam
- 2 slices sharp cheddar cheese
- Butter

Instructions:

1. Butter one side of each bread slice.
2. Spread peach jam on the unbuttered side of one slice.
3. Layer cheese on top of jam, then cover with the other slice, butter side out.
4. Grill on medium heat until bread is golden and cheese melted.

Southern Style Cheese-Stuffed Waffles

Ingredients:

- 2 cups waffle batter (prepared)
- 1 cup shredded cheddar cheese
- ½ cup cooked bacon bits (optional)

Instructions:

1. Preheat waffle iron.
2. Pour half the batter onto waffle iron.
3. Sprinkle cheese (and bacon) over batter, then cover with remaining batter.
4. Cook until golden and cheese is melted inside.

Buttermilk and Cheese Drop Biscuits

Ingredients:

- 2 cups self-rising flour
- 1 cup shredded cheddar cheese
- 1 cup buttermilk
- ¼ cup melted butter

Instructions:

1. Preheat oven to 425°F (220°C).
2. Mix flour and cheese in a bowl.
3. Stir in buttermilk until just combined.
4. Drop spoonfuls onto baking sheet.
5. Brush tops with melted butter.
6. Bake 12-15 minutes until golden.

Pimento Cheese-Stuffed Mushrooms

Ingredients:

- 12 large mushrooms, stems removed
- 1 cup pimento cheese
- ¼ cup breadcrumbs
- 2 tbsp chopped parsley

Instructions:

1. Preheat oven to 375°F (190°C).
2. Stuff mushrooms with pimento cheese.
3. Sprinkle breadcrumbs on top.
4. Bake 15-20 minutes until mushrooms are tender and topping is golden.
5. Garnish with parsley.

Cheese and Sausage Breakfast Grits Bake

Ingredients:

- 2 cups cooked grits
- 1 cup cooked breakfast sausage, crumbled
- 1 cup shredded cheddar cheese
- 3 eggs
- ½ cup milk
- Salt and pepper

Instructions:

1. Preheat oven to 350°F (175°C).
2. In a bowl, beat eggs and milk.
3. Stir in grits, sausage, cheese, salt, and pepper.
4. Pour into greased baking dish.
5. Bake 30-35 minutes until set and golden on top.

www.ingramcontent.com/pod-product-compliance
Lightning Source LLC
LaVergne TN
LVHW081323060526
838201LV00055B/2431